I0606345

Rad Riddles

Joe King

Abdo Kids Junior
is an Imprint of Abdo Kids
abdobooks.com

Abdo
ABDO KIDS JOKES
Kids

abdobooks.com

Published by Abdo Kids, a division of ABDO, P.O. Box 398166, Minneapolis, Minnesota 55439.

Printed in the United States of America, North Mankato, Minnesota.

052023

092023

Photo Credits: Getty Images, Shutterstock

Production Contributors: Teddy Borth, Jennie Forsberg, Grace Hansen

Design Contributors: Candice Keimig, Pakou Moua

Library of Congress Control Number: 2022946707

Publisher's Cataloging-in-Publication Data

Names: King, Joe, author.

Title: Rad riddles / by Joe King

Description: Minneapolis, Minnesota : Abdo Kids, 2024 | Series: Abdo kids jokes | Includes online resources and index.

Identifiers: ISBN 9781098266097 (lib. bdg.) | ISBN 9781098266790 (ebook) | ISBN 9781098267148 (Read-to-me ebook)

Subjects: LCSH: Jokes--Juvenile literature. | Wit and humor--Juvenile literature. | Riddles--Juvenile literature. | Humor--Juvenile literature.

Classification: DDC 818.6--dc23

Table of Contents

Rad Riddles

What goes up but never comes down?

Your age.

I'm tall when I'm young,
and I'm short when I'm old.
What am I?

A candle.

How many seconds are in a year?

12.

This riddle is a bit dated, don't you think?

What can you hold in your left hand but not in your right hand?

Your right elbow.

What can you hear, but not see or touch, even though you control it?

Your voice.

When things go wrong, what can you always count on?

Your fingers!

What can jump higher than a building?

Anything that can jump! Buildings don't jump, silly!

I'm as light as a feather, yet most people can't hold me for more than 2 minutes. What am I?

Breath.

Which is heavier, a ton of bricks or a ton of feathers?
They weigh the same!
HA!
This is a TON OF FUN!

If you don't keep me, I'll break. What am I?

A promise.

Kate's mother has three children: Snap, Crackle, and ___?

Kate!

I have keys, but no locks.
I have space, but no room.
You can enter but can't go
inside. What am I?
A keyboard.
Gotta pupdate my
Facebark page.

What can you catch,
but not throw?

A cold.

What has legs,
but can't walk?

A table.

What can run but never walk, has a mouth but never talks, has a head but never weeps, has a bed but never sleeps?

A river.

What is easy to get into and hard to get out of?

Trouble.

What gets wet while drying?

A towel.

What has a head and a tail but no body?

A coin.

What kind of room has
no doors or windows?

A mushroom.

Everyone has me but no one
can lose me. What am I?

A shadow.

What is orange and green and sounds like a parrot?
A carrot!
Polly want a carrot cake!
WHA!?

What gets bigger the more you take away?

A hole.

I am an odd number. Take away a letter and I become even. What number am I?

Seven.

A cowboy rode into town on Friday. He stayed for three nights and rode out on Friday. How is this possible?
His horse's name is Friday.
SALOON
SHERIFF
If the horseshoe fits!

I can be cracked or played, told or made. What am I?

A joke!

If you drop me, I'm sure to crack, but smile at me and I'll smile back. What am I?

A mirror.

What must be broken before you can use it?

An egg!

Joke-Telling Tips!

- Know your audience
- Timing is everything
- Confidence is key
- Go out on a high note!

Glossary

pun
a joke using a word that sounds like a different word or has another meaning. Examples from this book are "yoke" (joke) and "cents" (sense).

mouth
the place where a river runs into a larger body of water.

weep
to show strong feelings by crying.

Index

Visit **abdokids.com** to access crafts, games, videos, and more!

Use Abdo Kids code

ARK6097

or scan this QR code!